TIME FOR KIDS

WILD WORK!

ANIMAL TRAINERS

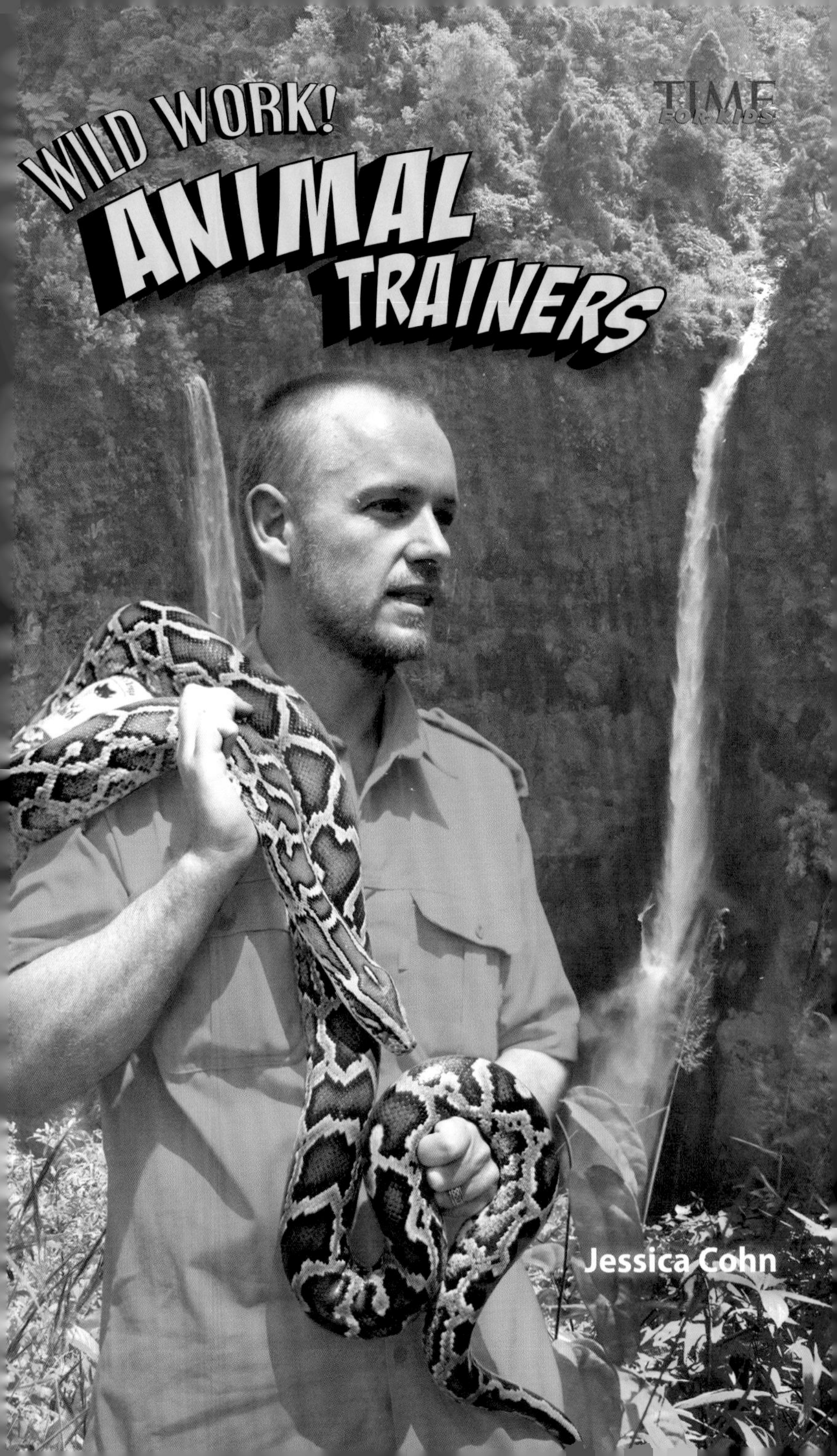

Jessica Cohn

Consultants

Timothy Rasinski, Ph.D.
Kent State University

Lori Oczkus
Literacy Consultant

Thorsten Pape
Animal Trainer

Based on writing from
TIME For Kids. TIME For Kids and the *TIME For Kids* logo are registered trademarks of TIME Inc. Used under license.

Publishing Credits

Dona Herweck Rice, *Editor-in-Chief*
Lee Aucoin, *Creative Director*
Jamey Acosta, *Senior Editor*
Heidi Fiedler, *Editor*
Lexa Hoang, *Designer*
Stephanie Reid, *Photo Editor*
Sandy Phan, *Contributing Author*
Rachelle Cracchiolo, *M.S.Ed., Publisher*

Image Credits: p.61 AGE fotostock; pp.18–19, 19, 35, 36 Associated Press; p.24 Circus World/Ringling Bros. and Barnum & Bailey; pp.24–25 William Woodcock Collection; pp.30–31 Christopher Schulz Collection; pp.30, 40–40, 57 Getty Images; p.46 ChinFotoPress/Newscom; p.52 Visual&Written/Newscom; p.40 EPA/Newscom; p.29 imagebroker/Raimund Kutter/Newscom; pp.48–49 Zuma Press/Newscom; pp.28–29 action press/Newscom; pp.50–51 (illustrations) Timothy J. Bradley; pp.32–33 (illustrations) J.J. Rudisill; pp.47, 49 U.S. Navy; pp.44, 44–45 WENN.com; All other images from Shutterstock.

Teacher Created Materials

5301 Oceanus Drive
Huntington Beach, CA 92649-1030
http://www.tcmpub.com

ISBN 978-1-4333-4942-3
© 2013 Teacher Created Materials, Inc.

TABLE OF CONTENTS

Amazing Feats 4

The Elephant in the Room 15

Big Cats 27

It's a Bear 37

In the Water 47

Risks and Rewards 55

Glossary 58

Index .60

Bibliography 62

More to Explore 63

About the Author 64

AMAZING FEATS

Animal trainers train animals to perform. They also teach animals such as **guide dogs** how to help people. Getting animals to respond to people is always at the heart of their work. Animal trainers take care of animals and understand **animal psychology**. They form close bonds with the animals they train. But the best trainers never forget that the animals they work with are wild creatures. They are always aware of the dangers of their job.

An elephant follows a trainer's directions to paint.

THINK LINK

➤ Why would someone want to become an animal trainer?

➤ What techniques do trainers use to influence an animal's behavior?

➤ How does someone prepare to become an animal trainer?

5

Creatures of Habit

Animals learn in two different ways. To understand the first way, think about a man that often orders pizza. When the doorbell rings, the man's dog starts drooling. Why? The dog has come to associate the bell with pizza. Drooling when the doorbell rings is a **response** beyond its control. This is an example of **classical conditioning**.

The man pays the delivery person and begins eating a slice of pizza. His dog jumps up and puts its paws on the table, whining and begging. The man tells it to sit. The dog sits quietly and earns a bite of crust. This is an outcome of **operant conditioning**. It is behavior the dog can learn and control.

To the Dogs

Ivan Pavlov was a famous researcher. He gave his dogs food and measured how much drool they made. Next, he began ringing a bell before feeding them. Eventually, the dogs drooled when hearing the bell, food or no food.

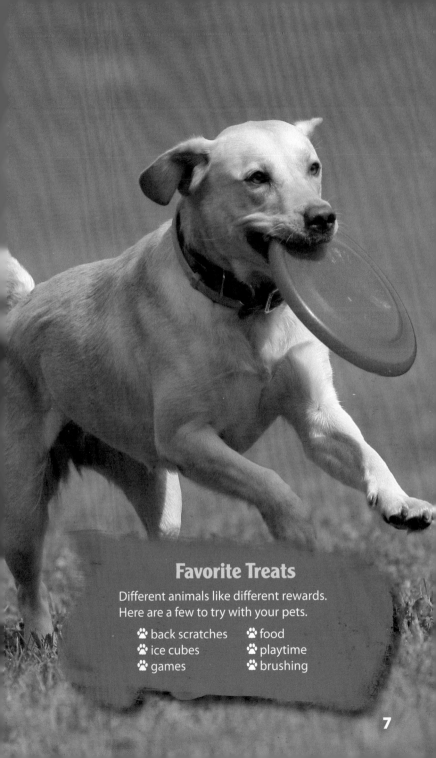

Favorite Treats

Different animals like different rewards.
Here are a few to try with your pets.

- 🐾 back scratches
- 🐾 ice cubes
- 🐾 games
- 🐾 food
- 🐾 playtime
- 🐾 brushing

Think Like a Trainer

Training any animal follows a pattern of stimulus, response, and **reinforcement**. The stimulus is a word or signal. The response is the desired behavior. The reinforcement is when the trainer lets the animal know that he or she recognizes the behavior. Trainers also use reinforcement to stop bad behaviors. They create a link between a behavior and a reward or a punishment.

Positive Reinforcement

Stimulus: The trainer gives the animal a signal.

Negative Reinforcement

Behavior: The animal does something bad.

STOP! THINK...

- What does *positive* mean in this chart?

- What does *negative* mean in this chart?

- Do you think animals respond better to rewards or punishments?

Response: The animal does something good.

Reinforcement: The trainer starts a fun activity or gives the animal a treat.

Response: The animal stops the bad behavior.

Reinforcement: The trainer takes away something good or stops doing something fun.

9

Indirect Instincts

Animals do things that feel good, even when they are punished for it. Many dogs love chewing things around the house. They often continue this behavior after repeated punishments. An owner may replace the chewed items with a toy. Then, the owner rewards the dog for playing with it. If the dog is busy with a toy, it won't have time to chew other things.

Animal trainers also replace bad behavior with different behaviors. For example, a parrot may scream loudly when people visit. Her trainer ignores it. Instead, the trainer gives the bird treats when she says "Welcome." The trainer has it perform an **incompatible behavior**. The parrot cannot scream and talk at the same time.

Extinction Burst

When a trainer changes his or her response to an unwanted behavior, the behavior may get worse before it stops. This is called an **extinction burst**. When a trainer starts ignoring a screaming bird, the bird may scream louder or more often for several days to get the trainer's attention. The bad behavior eventually stops if the trainer consistently ignores it. The bird will choose other behaviors that result in positive attention.

10

Bridging Behaviors

Trainers sometimes use a clicker, whistle, word, or touch to let an animal know it is doing something right. A trainer may blow a whistle right after a dolphin flips. The dolphin may be underwater or far away from the trainer. The whistle lets the dolphin know the exact behavior to repeat. The whistle is also a bridge between the right behavior and the treat or reward the dolphin will receive later. Sometimes, the whistle alone is a reward for work well done.

Training Is Caring

All training starts with caregiving. A well-trained animal is comfortable and healthy. Trainers spend lots of time feeding, cleaning, and grooming animals. They clean the animals' living areas. They also keep health and hygiene records. They make sure the animals get enough exercise. This is a time for trainers to earn the animals' trust. Many trainers serve as caregivers for years before they start training animals.

Pay and Perks

Animal training is not known for making people rich. Beginning trainers often take a second job to make more income.

Training the Trainer

Zoos and aquariums often require trainers to take **biology** and **marine ecology** classes. They help trainers understand where and how animals like to live.

On Their Terms

Sometimes, it may seem that an animal thinks it's human. A dog may eat human food, sit with its owners, and make human-like noises. But dogs actually think humans are dogs. They take cues from humans the way they do from other dogs. Other animals view humans in the same way. They may understand that we are not quite elephants or tigers, but that's the closest thing they know.

Help Wanted!
Elephant Trainer

Requirements

The ideal candidate has a degree in **zoology** or similar studies. A certificate from an animal training school is a plus. He or she has worked with large animals at places such as wildlife parks or horse stables. Trainers must be firm, patient , positive, and confident.

14

THE ELEPHANT
IN THE ROOM

It is one thing to train house cats or dogs. They are smaller than people. And they know who is boss. But elephants weigh between two and seven tons. Their trainers must be very skilled and careful. Many elephants are trained from a young age to get used to human contact. This makes it easier for people to care for them as they get bigger.

Trained elephants are primarily Asian elephants, not to be confused with the much larger African elephants.

ASIAN   AFRICAN

How can you tell? Asian and African elephants each have ears shaped a little like the continents they come from.

A Tradition of Training

In India, the people who train elephants are called **mahouts**. The know-how needed to train elephants is passed down through families. The mahouts are highly respected. They understand that elephants run in herds. The animals expect to be dominated by a leader. So trainers establish themselves as the leaders. Once they do, the elephants follow them. The trained elephants are treated as part of the mahouts' families.

Elephant God

Ganesh, or Ganesha, is a **Hindu** god with an elephant head. He is believed to be the god of new beginnings. His large ears show he listens to his worshippers' prayers. Ganesh's elephant trunk symbolizes his strength and ability to do things very precisely.

Sizes Side by Side

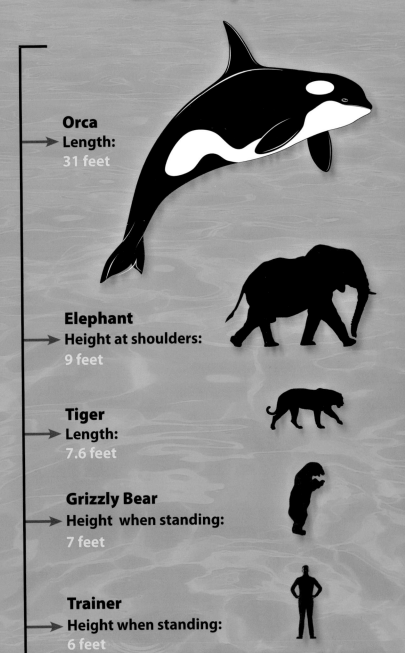

Orca
Length:
31 feet

Elephant
Height at shoulders:
9 feet

Tiger
Length:
7.6 feet

Grizzly Bear
Height when standing:
7 feet

Trainer
Height when standing:
6 feet

What's It Worth?

Reports show that animal trainers report higher numbers of work-related injuries than other workers. But trainers, who tend to be animal lovers, believe that being with animals is worth the risk.

The Big and Small of It

No one can lift an elephant, so elephants must be trained to cooperate with keepers. The elephant must learn to move so others can wash it and give it medicine. It must allow doctors to examine its feet and other body parts.

Huge Risks

Working with large animals comes with some big risks. In 2011, a trainer died at the Knoxville Zoo in Tennessee. She was killed by an elephant in her care. The 8,000-pound animal backed into a wall and crushed her. Successful trainers never forget the risks of the job. They understand that animals are not humans. They also know an animal's limitations. A trainer does not ask an animal to do things it cannot do or things that would harm it. In the past, some trainers treated animals cruelly. But today, nearly all trainers understand kindness is more powerful. And it's the right way to treat animals.

Guide to Elephants

Most trainers avoid physical punishment. They use physical communication instead. For example, a trainer might touch an elephant behind the knee with a guide. A guide is a long pole with a hook on the end. It's annoying to the elephant but not painful.

Big Jobs

In the Roman Empire, elephants carried rich people great distances. The animals also took soldiers and supplies into battle. In India, elephants were called to duty as late as World War II. Asian elephants also worked on farms and in logging.

Today, there is no call for war elephants. But people still teach elephants to clear trees in Asia. Most animal trainers work in animal parks. The trainers help the elephants stay healthy. They also prepare them to take part in scientific studies.

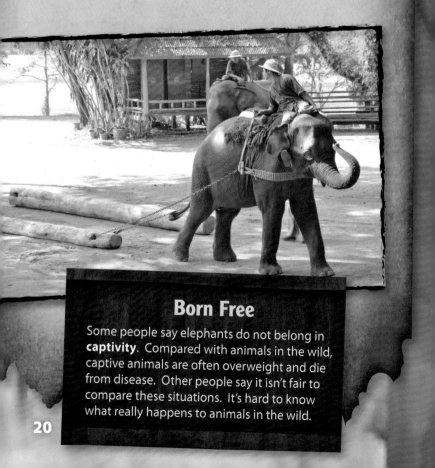

Born Free

Some people say elephants do not belong in **captivity**. Compared with animals in the wild, captive animals are often overweight and die from disease. Other people say it isn't fair to compare these situations. It's hard to know what really happens to animals in the wild.

Big Issues

Even in the wild, elephants need protection. There are fewer than 50,000 Asian elephants left in nature. Many were killed for their tusks. Others lost living areas as people took over the land. Zoos often take in elephants to prevent them from being **culled**.

The trunk of an elephant has over 40,000 muscles. Elephants use their trunks like a hand to hold objects, scratch themselves, and shake trunks in greeting.

Talking the Talk

Animal trainers must learn how animals communicate with each other. Elephants use 70 sounds and 160 different gestures and expressions to communicate. There are squeals, cries, screams, roars, snorts, rumbles, and groans. Their sounds can show anger, joy, playfulness, and a wide range of other emotions. Humans are only just beginning to learn all the ways they communicate.

A powerful vibration can mean "Hello! Are you there?" Elephants lift their heads and spread their ears to hear the answer. They also often lift a foot off the ground to detect vibrations.

Sounds can coordinate the way elephants move in a group.

Some elephant sounds are too low for humans to hear. In the wild, elephants can hear other elephants from over a mile away.

The calls can be as soft as a whisper or louder than a jackhammer.

Elephants show they want to play by stretching their head down and folding their trunk under or around their tusks.

Folding the ears or tossing the head can mean the elephant is becoming aggressive.

A long rumble says "I want to go in this direction. Let's go together." It can last five to six seconds and be repeated roughly every minute.

Elephants often freeze in place when they are listening to or smelling something unfamiliar.

Ben Williams

One of the most famous elephant trainers of all time was Ben Williams. He performed with elephants for half a century. Williams was raised in a circus family. By age six, he was performing. Four generations of performers preceded him on his mother's side. And both his father and stepfather worked with elephants, too.

Even as a toddler, Williams jumped from the back of one elephant to another. In one of his popular circus acts, he lay on the ground. He allowed the elephants to come close to crushing him. The crowds went wild when his elephant spun him around.

Anna May

Williams worked with an elephant named Anna May for 49 years. The Big Apple Circus dropped their elephant act in 2000. Williams loved Anna May. "She makes me look good," Williams told the *New York Times*. "She's forgotten more tricks than I know."

Bad Surprise

Trainers know that even a well-trained elephant is a dangerous animal. In 1982, Anna May accidentally killed a woman who entered her trailer by surprise. The incident nearly ended Williams's career.

25

Help Wanted!
Big-Cat Trainer

Requirements

The ideal big-cat trainer has a degree in animal management or similar studies. A trainer must go through step-by-step direct training with the animals. These creatures are at the top of their food chains. A trainer must understand their biology and behavior.

BIG CATS

Most cat owners don't bother teaching their cats much beyond how to use the litter box. But zoos need to teach their big cats to cooperate and live in captivity. Lions and tigers are moody, which makes their training difficult. They're often independent animals, though lions are fairly social.

Big cats of all kinds are a big challenge. They become aggressive during feeding time and must be handled carefully. A male lion can make a kill very quickly. Like small cats, big cats have fast reflexes. They may attack playfully and never realize that anything went wrong.

When tigers like someone, they let the person know by making a *chuff* sound. Then, they use their noses to point toward the person they like.

Fierce Competition

The competition among big-cat trainers is fierce, much like the competition among the animals themselves. An **internship** program may pick only a few people out of hundreds. Applicants must go through intense interviews that may last several days before they can begin training.

Keeping Up

Big cat trainers must stay in excellent physical and mental shape. They need strength and speed to keep up with the animals in their care.

A Wild Lifestyle

Each cat **species** and individual animal is different. It takes a long time to win over these wild creatures. It is said that training exotic animals is more a lifestyle than a job. New trainers may spend years watching and helping another trainer. Cats need care and feeding at all hours.

People who train big cats get degrees in subjects related to animals and wildlife management. They may study zoology or biology. Then, they seek internships in animal parks or wildlife refuges. Some work with big cats in labs and field research.

Teamwork

Working with cats outside a cage requires a team of highly skilled people. Backup trainers control crowds and pay attention to possible problems. They let trainers know about any trouble and help when needed. Trainers need backup because they must focus completely on the cats to avoid accidents.

Roar of the Crowd

Many circus animal trainers must be entertainers as well as animal experts. They may wear bright costumes. Some hold hoops that tigers or lions jump through. Others perform comedy acts in which an animal appears to trip or shove them. Any animal trainer on stage needs strong **showmanship** skills. He or she must be able to hold an audience in suspense before a trick. Circus trainers make people laugh or feel as if they know the animals.

Cruel or Caring?

Many **animal rights** groups believe that animals are treated cruelly in the circus. Until the 1970s, many circus trainers beat and whipped their animals. However, today's circuses care for their animals with kindness and train them with rewards.

Killer Show

Years ago, big-cat performances played up the danger of a killer cat in action. Today, the shows tend to show off a trainer's relationship with the cats, yet the danger is as real as ever. As one trainer put it, "Trained cats are rare."

Food for Thought

With cats, using food as a reward can cause problems. The cats' drive to eat is strong, and the animals are powerful. Food can be too distracting. Trainers must try to get the animals to respond to commands and sounds instead of food.

31

Battling Boredom

Animals in the wild spend much of their time catching prey or staying away from **predators**. Life in an animal park or other controlled space is very different from life in the wild. Animal trainers need to make sure animals don't become bored. A restless animal may become aggressive or sick.

Animals stay active with games and creative activities.

Trainers make animals "hunt" for their food.

Instead of barred cages and cement walls, zoos try to make natural-looking homes for animals.

Animals must solve problems to get to their food.

Animals play with different toys.

33

Siegfried and Roy

Around the world, they are known simply by their first names. Siegfried Fischbacher and Roy Horn both grew up in Germany. Siegfried had a love of magic. Roy loved animals. The two met while working on the ocean liner where Siegfried performed small magic shows.

Many say Roy smuggled a cheetah onboard. To spice up his magic act, Siegfried brought the animal on stage. The show was a hit! The duo went on to develop a multimillion-dollar magic show with animals in Las Vegas. With the profits, Siegfried and Roy created an organization to save the **endangered** royal white tiger.

Tragedy Strikes

Roy trained his cats with **affection bonding**. To earn their trust, he slept in the same bed with them until they were one year old. But trust only goes so far with a big cat. In October 2003, Roy stumbled on stage. In response, one of his white tigers bit him in the neck.

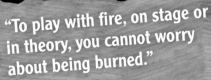

> "To play with fire, on stage or in theory, you cannot worry about being burned."
> —Siegfried Fischbacher, magician and animal trainer

No Blame

The tiger's attack nearly killed Roy, and he was paralyzed. Yet neither he nor his partner blamed the cat. The cat, they said, was just being a cat. The same tiger had performed 2,000 times without a problem.

Help Wanted!

Bear Trainer

Requirements

Jobs with **accredited** institutions usually require a degree in a related subject. Bear trainers often have previous experience working with large animals, such as horses. Bear trainers are team players who are patient, positive, confident, and in good health.

IT'S A BEAR

Lions, tigers, and bears—they are known as some of the most frightening creatures on Earth. But even bears can be trained. They have been for centuries. The Ursari people in Eastern Europe became famous for training bears. They traveled from place to place, making their bears perform tricks for money.

More recently, *Animal Planet* aired a TV show called *Growing Up Grizzly*. The show starred three grizzlies named Tank, Little Bart, and Honey-Bump. It followed their adventures with trainers Lynne and Doug Seus. The Seuses helped the bears prepare to appear in movies. They taught them how to deal with traffic, noise, and other distractions. Other trainers prepare bears to cooperate with keepers in zoos and animal parks. Some trainers help bears follow simple commands. They clean the animals and their living areas. They keep records about the bears' care.

The Seuses feed their bears with different bowls and at different times. That way, the bears don't get too used to a routine. A change in routine would cause the bears stress.

Wild Animal Actors

Mark and Dawn Dumas, a Canadian couple, own a company that trains animal actors. They work with Agee, the only trained polar bear in North America. He lies down, crawls, and sits for them. Agee's actions appear natural on camera. But it takes a lot of work behind the scenes. Polar bears are the largest land predators. And Agee would likely harm anyone other than the Dumases.

Bears are powerful creatures. Working with them involves many risks. Not long ago, a trainer was killed at a wild animal center. One minute the bear was licking the man's face. The next moment the bear was biting into his neck.

Home on the Range

All bears are on the list of endangered species. Using their fame from appearing on *Animal Planet*, the Seuses raised money for bears in the wild. They have paid to protect areas in northern Idaho and northwestern Montana, keeping them safe for the bears to use.

spectacled bear

Bears of the World

There are eight types of bears. The most famous are the grizzly bear, the American black bear, and the polar bear. There are also sloth bears, Asiatic black bears, and giant pandas. The sun bear in India has a sunny orange marking on its chest. The spectacled bear has markings that look like eyeglasses. It lives in South America.

Save the Bears

Some of the most rewarding work for bear trainers is **rehabilitation**. Many trainers help sick and injured animals recover. One of the more dramatic stories comes from India, where trainers are teaching bears how to be wild again.

Some tribes in Asia teach bears to dance and collect coins for performances. The bears are taken from the wild as cubs. Their teeth are knocked out. A hole is poked through their snouts, where a rope is attached. In India, the toothless bears are being saved and taken to safety. Trainers teach them to climb trees and look for termites, which the bears like to eat. The training makes it possible for them to live freely again.

Black-bear cubs love to play. Orphaned cubs at rehabilitation centers may chase each other around chairs or compete for control of a swimming pool.

End of the Dance

India made bear dancing illegal in 1972. Since then, hundreds of bears have been sent to a **sanctuary**. The people who used to rely on the bears for money are being trained to do other things. In 2009, India made history by taking the last of its dancing bears off the streets.

Dentists are called in to treat bears that are missing teeth. Rescued bears are fed tasty fruits, porridge, and honey, their favorite treat.

41

Called to Help

If you love animals and are interested in becoming a trainer, volunteering is a good way to see what this kind of work is like. Spend time at zoos, aquariums, and rehabilitation centers, and get to know the workers. Look for internships and volunteer programs that will welcome your interest in animals.

Formal training is just part of the preparation to become an animal trainer. This job requires quick thinking and common sense. As with all animal jobs, a positive attitude, patience, and a love of animals are a plus.

Do you have what it takes? Ask yourself:

- Do I have physical strength?
- Do I have emotional strength?
- Do I keep a positive attitude?
- Do I take the time to learn things and show others how to do them?
- Am I good at solving problems in my daily life?
- Do I communicate well with people and animals?
- Am I willing to start at a low level and work my way up?

42

If being an animal trainer sounds interesting, but isn't quite right for you, consider these other lines of work.

🐾 become a veterinarian

🐾 study the ocean and other places animals lives

🐾 conduct research in animal biology

🐾 work for animal conservation groups

Casey Anderson

Casey Anderson is a famous bear trainer. After college, Anderson worked as an animal keeper. Then, he became a trainer. His best friend is a bear named Brutus. He has raised the bear since it was a baby.

Brutus was a baby grizzly born in a park overpopulated with bears. To save the cub, Anderson created a bear reserve in Montana. Today, Brutus roams there. He appears with Anderson to teach the public about the need for grizzly conservation. The two have been featured in a TV series called *Expedition Wild*. It explores the needs of wildlife in Yellowstone National Park.

Brutus was an important part of Anderson's wedding. He was the best man!

Grizzly Encounter

Anderson founded the Montana Grizzly Encounter in 2004 for grizzlies that need rescuing. The center teaches that the bears are wild and belong in the wild. Anderson tells audiences that aside from Brutus, people should never get close to a bear.

Brutus the Bear

Brutus is close to 900 pounds now. Though he spends most of his time on the reserve, he sometimes travels to do commercials. Brutus made an appearance on *The Oprah Show* in 2009.

Help Wanted!

Marine Mammal Training

Requirements

Must be able to train dolphins, whales, seals, sea lions, walruses, and other animals to interact with humans. Ideal applicants will be able to teach behaviors that educate and entertain audiences as needed. Veterinary training or a degree in marine biology (or similar subject) is required. Public speaking skills are a plus for some positions.

IN THE WATER

It's hard to think of a more exotic place to work than in the water. **Marine biologists** study plants and animals in the water. Some study **organisms** too small to be seen with human eyes. Others research fish and larger creatures.

Marine mammal trainers also spend a lot of time underwater. They often have the same interests as marine biologists. Trainers usually work with larger mammals such as dolphins and whales. Trainers often take part in research. They study the behaviors of the most intelligent sea creatures. But their main job is to care for the animals.

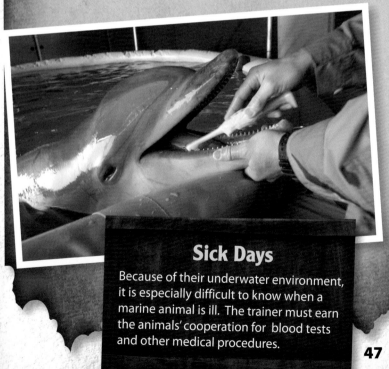

Sick Days

Because of their underwater environment, it is especially difficult to know when a marine animal is ill. The trainer must earn the animals' cooperation for blood tests and other medical procedures.

Animal Miracle Worker

One of the most famous animal trainers is Abby Stone. She is known for her work with a dolphin named Winter. When she was young, Winter was caught in a trap. Her tail fins were hurt. No one expected her to live very long. But Stone fed and held her for hours in the water. Winter was given a **prosthetic** tail, and Stone trained her to wear it. They started slowly—just a few minutes a day. Now, Winter can swim easily with the tail. She inspired and starred in the film *Dolphin Tale*.

Dolphin Divers

Dolphins are some of the most popular animals to work with. These **cetaceans** are intelligent and curious. They enjoy working with humans. The United States Navy has trained them to find objects lost underwater. They also guard boats, bring equipment to divers, and carry cameras. Dolphins are admired for their creativity. They become bored easily and will invent new tricks for their amusement. They like a variety of rewards. Some dolphins enjoy back rubs. Others like playing with toys or going for a swim with their trainer.

Trainers spend time learning what each dolphin prefers. During these play sessions and feedings, the dolphins also come to know the trainers. If a trainer is a loud, excited person, the dolphin may become loud and excited as well. If the trainer does something the dolphin doesn't like, the dolphin may simply ignore the trainer. Sometimes, it's not clear who is training who!

Men stationed at a Navy base in Gulfport, Mississippi, play with a rescued dolphin.

Very Tricky

Before you could learn to read, you had to learn the alphabet. Then, you had to learn simple words. Only then could you read full sentences. Just like you, an animal learns things step by step. When animal trainers teach an animal a new trick, they break down the trick into steps.

1 The trainer shows the dolphin a new hand signal for the high-jump.

6 The dolphin gets a treat and lots of love from its trainer.

2 The trainer touches the dolphin with a **target**. Then, she blows a whistle to let the dolphin know it did something right.

3 The dolphin follows the target and moves to touch it on its own. The trainer blows a whistle.

4 The trainer raises the target higher and higher above the water.

5 The trainer gives the high-jump hand signal. The dolphin gracefully leaps high up into the air.

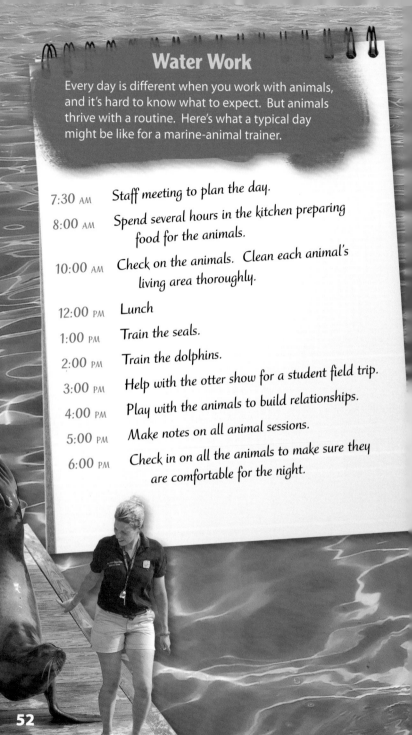

Water Work

Every day is different when you work with animals, and it's hard to know what to expect. But animals thrive with a routine. Here's what a typical day might be like for a marine-animal trainer.

7:30 AM	Staff meeting to plan the day.
8:00 AM	Spend several hours in the kitchen preparing food for the animals.
10:00 AM	Check on the animals. Clean each animal's living area thoroughly.
12:00 PM	Lunch
1:00 PM	Train the seals.
2:00 PM	Train the dolphins.
3:00 PM	Help with the otter show for a student field trip.
4:00 PM	Play with the animals to build relationships.
5:00 PM	Make notes on all animal sessions.
6:00 PM	Check in on all the animals to make sure they are comfortable for the night.

Training Trainers

Many trainers have college degrees. Some even have advanced degrees. They study subjects related to animal management.

It is also important for trainers to join groups such as the International Marine Animal Trainers Association (IMATA). This group posts job openings, news, and events. Potential trainers also attend events to meet people who may be able to help them find work. Trainers must stay on top of what is new in the field. They talk with other trainers to learn what's working well for them.

Marine-animal trainers must pass difficult swimming and diving tests.

A trainer shows off by relaxing under an elephant.

RISKS AND REWARDS

An animal trainer's job is wild work! Training large or aggressive animals comes with the risk of injury or even death. It takes years of preparation to become a trainer. Many trainers have degrees in biology or animal science. They work long hours to make sure animals are safe and healthy. But most trainers will tell you they love their jobs. They believe the hard work and danger are worth it. These brave and caring trainers show us animals are capable of amazing things. Most of all, they remind us to respect and care for the animals that do so much for us.

The Real Deal

Writer Jessica Cohn sat down with Ken Ramirez of Chicago's Shedd Aquarium. With over 35 years of animal care and training experience, he knows just how wild this work can get.

Jessica: How did you get started as an animal trainer?

Ken: [In high school], I volunteered with a guide-dog organization. [In college], I focused on animal behavior as a major. [That led to becoming a] trainer in a marine life park. Most of what I learned was gathered from more experienced trainers and working with the animals every day.

Jessica: It sounds like you've always been passionate about animals.

Ken: Animals deserve the best care we can possibly provide. Training should not be considered a luxury that is only provided if there is time—it is an essential part of good animal care.

Jessica: What advice would you give to someone who wants to become an animal trainer?

Ken: Focus on any area that is of interest to you: biology, marine biology, zoology, animal behavior, **environmental science**, etc. [In the end], you will learn how to train from the experience of doing it. [But] the degree can be [key to] landing many jobs and will be [helpful]. Gain practical experience anywhere that you can. At the beginning, you should be willing to take any type of animal work. Once you have [found your focus], join professional organizations that focus on training [or] the species that interests you. [Many] have student memberships. [These] allow you to learn about the profession, keep track of **trends**, and learn about job opportunities.

Ramirez shows a visitor how he cares for a penguin.

Ramirez works with a sea lion.

GLOSSARY

accredited—certified as meeting a standard of excellence

affection bonding—the process of earning an animal's trust through close and constant positive contact

animal psychology—the study of the mental processes that control animal behavior

animal rights—the idea that animals should be respected and protected from abuse by humans

biology—the study of or science of life

captivity—a place where animals are held and prevented from escaping

cetaceans—all aquatic mammals

classical conditioning—behavior training in which a behavior is associated with something else

culled—reduced or cut in numbers by hunting or killing

endangered—in danger of dying out

environmental science—the study of natural communities and how they form and survive

extinction burst—when an animal's behavior gets worse before it gets better

guide dogs—dogs that help people with limited sight get around

Hindu—a person who follows a set of social, cultural, and religious beliefs and practices native to India

incompatible behavior—a behavior that cannot be done at the same time as another behavior

internship—a program that teaches students under supervision in an on-the-job setting

mahouts—traditional elephant trainers of India

marine biologists—scientists who study life in the sea

marine ecology—the study of habitats in the water

operant conditioning—behavior training in which a behavior occurs in response to reward or punishment

organisms—independent living things of all kinds

prosthetic—related to an artificial or mechanical device that is worn to replace a missing or an injured limb

rehabilitation—the restoration of health

reinforcement—a thing that supports or assists an action

response—a reaction to a stimulus

sanctuary—a place that is safe

showmanship—a special skill for presenting something in a dramatic way

species—a class of living things with common features

stimulus—a thing that influences an activity

target—a training tool used with marine animals; usually a small float at the end of a long pole

trends—the ways things go or the developing style of things

zoology—the study and science of animals

INDEX

African elephants, 15
Agee, 38
American black bear, 39
Anderson, Casey, 44
animal psychology, 4
Animal Planet, 37–38
Anna May, 24–25
Asia, 20, 40
Asian elephants, 15
Asiatic black bear, 39
bear, 37–41, 44–45
Big Apple Circus, 24
biology, 13, 26, 29, 43, 46, 55–56
Brutus, 45
Canadian, 38
cetaceans, 49
dog, 4, 6, 10, 13, 15, 56
Dolphin Tale, 48
dolphin, 8, 11, 46–52
Dumas, Dawn, 38
Dumas, Mark, 38
Eastern Europe, 37
elephants, 4, 14–25, 54
Expedition Wild, 44
Fischbacher, Siegfried, 34–35
Ganesh, 16

giant panda, 39
grizzly bear, 17, 39
Growing Up Grizzly, 37
guide dogs, 4
Hindu, 16
Honey-Bump, 37
Horn, Roy, 34
India, 16, 20, 39–41
International Marine
    Animal Trainers
    Association
    (IMATA), 53
Knoxville Zoo, 19
lions, 27, 30, 34, 37
Little Bart, 37
marine biologists, 47
marine mammals, 46–47
Montana Grizzly
    Encounter, 45
Montana, 38, 44
New York Times, 24
North America, 38
Oprah Show, The 45
orca, 17
parrot, 10
Pavlov, Ivan, 6
pets, 7
polar bear, 38–39

prosthetic tail, 48
Ramirez, Ken, 56
Roman Empire, 20
sea lion, 46, 57
Seus, Doug, 37
Seus, Lynne, 37
Shedd Aquarium, 56
sloth bear, 39
South America, 39
spectacled bear, 39
Stone, Abby, 48
sun bear, 39
Tank, 37

Tennessee, 19
tigers, 13, 17, 27, 30, 34,
    37
United States Navy, 49
Ursari, 37
Williams, Ben, 24
Winter, 48
World War II, 20
Yellowstone National
    Park, 44
zoology, 14, 29, 56
zoos, 13, 21, 27, 33, 37,
    42

BIBLIOGRAPHY

Davey, Pete. *A Dolphin in Front of You.*
Ocean Publishing, 2005.

Find out what it takes to be a dolphin trainer from an expert.
With tips and tricks only insiders know, this book will help you
know what to expect in this career, build a resume, and practice
interviewing as well as discuss the schooling that will help you
pursue a wildly fun career as a dolphin trainer.

Goldish, Meish. *Dolphins in the Navy (America's
Animal Soldiers).* Bearport Publishing, 2012.

Learn how the United States Navy has trained dolphins.
This book is full of pictures and stories of the duties K-Dog the
dolphin has performed to keep his country safe. That's one
brave dolphin!

Hansen, Sherry and Brad Steiger. *The Mysteries
of Animal Intelligence: True Stories of Animals with
Amazing Abilities.* Tor Books, 2007.

You wouldn't believe all the amazing animal feats in this book.
From a dolphin saving a drowning person to a cat defending
a baby from a rattlesnake, it is one crazy–but true–story
after another.

Pang, Evelyn and Hilary Louie. *Good Dog!
Kids Teach Kids About Dog Behavior and Training.*
Dogwise Publishing, 2008.

It's never too late to train your dog. Learn how to communicate
better with your dog with fun training techniques. You can
share the tips with your parents as well.

MORE TO
EXPLORE

Beyond Just Bears
http://www.beyondbears.ca

Find out more about Mark and Dawn Dumas's dream of training animal actors. They have provided animals for hundreds of television shows, movies, and commercials. Get to know a handful of their "stars," and check out the impressive roster of roles.

Dolphin Research Center
http://www.dolphins.org/marineed_trainingDRC.php

Many people dream of training dolphins. At the Dolphin Research Center, that dream can become reality. Learn why and how this center trains its dolphins, and get to know the personalities of the pod. Click on the kids area under the *Marine Education* tab, where you'll find fun facts, games, and coloring pages.

Science Buddies: Animal Trainer
http://www.sciencebuddies.org/

Type *Animal Trainer* in the top-right-hand search box. Here, you'll learn all sorts of things about becoming an animal trainer. Recommended schooling, interviews with professionals, and project ideas are just the beginning. Click *On the Job* to watch a video and get a better idea of what animal trainers really do.

Zoological Park Careers
http://www.seaworld.org/career-resources/info-books/zoo-careers/index.htm

This site has lots of information for aspiring animal trainers. You'll find all kinds of practical information about schools with specialized programs, different types of animal training, and more books to help you explore the many options available.

ABOUT THE AUTHOR

Jessica Cohn grew up in Michigan. She has a bachelor's degree in English and a master's in written communications. She has worked in educational publishing for more than a decade as a writer and an editor. During that time, she has written articles and books on many subjects, including careers. She is married and has two sons. Her family is based in New York state, with a smart old dog who will do tricks only when he's on comfortable carpeting.